the
untethered soul

GUIDED
JOURNAL

PRACTICES TO JOURNEY
BEYOND YOURSELF

MICHAEL A. SINGER

NEW HARBINGER PUBLICATIONS, INC.
INSTITUTE OF NOETIC SCIENCES

PUBLISHER'S NOTE

A copublication of New Harbinger Publications and Institute of Noetic Sciences.

The Untethered Soul is a registered trademark of Shanti Publications, Inc.

Printed in China

Distributed in Canada by Raincoast Books

Copyright © 2020 by Michael A. Singer

New Harbinger Publications, Inc.

5674 Shattuck Avenue

Oakland, CA 94609

www.newharbinger.com

Journal prompts coauthored by Catharine Meyers

Cover and interior design by Amy Shoup
Cover illustration of horse by Sara Christian
Illustration elements by Julia Dreams, Awa Marc, Lisima, and Basia Stryjecka at creativemarket.com

Acquired by Catharine Meyers

Library of Congress Cataloging-in-Publication Data
on file with publisher

22   21

10   9   8   7   6   5   4   3   2

CONTENTS

INTRODUCTION

TAKE A GUIDED JOURNEY TO YOUR INNERMOST SELF

"There is nothing more important to true growth than realizing you are not the voice of the mind — you are the one who hears it."

—MICHAEL A. SINGER

When I sat down to write *The Untethered Soul*, the intention behind the book was very simple: I wanted to share a path to complete inner freedom with anyone willing to receive it. Spiritual growth should be simple, clear, and intuitively obvious. Freedom is the most natural thing in the world—it is, in fact, our birthright. The problem is that we obscure this simple truth with our mind, emotions, and preferences. *The Untethered Soul* takes us on a journey in which we directly experience the innate truths within us. We discover who we are by letting go of who we are not. This deep inner journey is not intended just for mystics or scholars; it is a journey back to the seat of Self, and it can be taken by anyone.

Now, we are pleased to offer this beautiful guided journal for *The Untethered Soul* as an ideal vehicle for facilitating your inner journey. Our intention is to guide you through a deeper understanding of your relationship to your mind, your emotions, and your inner energies. You'll explore releasing the noisy mind and letting go of difficult past experiences you've held within yourself. By doing so, you can access the freedom and happiness of your true innermost Self that is witnessing it all.

Each journal entry contains one of the most powerful passages from the text of *The Untethered Soul*. The prompts that follow each passage encourage you to fully relate the teaching to your personal experiences. This allows you to dive deeper into the essence of the teaching and to make it part of your daily life. In some cases, the prompts lead you into further contemplation and introspection. In other cases, exercises are given to help deepen your practice. Since expressing your own relationship to a teaching helps to deepen your understanding of it, space is provided to write and reflect upon your personal experiences. That is the purpose of this journal: to take you beyond the power of the words into the power of direct experience.

You are about to embark on a journey beyond yourself to inner freedom, happiness, and self-realization. As you read, reflect, and write, you'll see these pages fill with the story of your personal awakening. You may choose to continue writing beyond the bounds of this book, in a separate journal. Or you may find that some passages lead you more to reflection than to writing. All of this is fine. Whatever your process, make this journal your own creation. At journey's end, you can always revisit the most resonant prompts, deepening your understanding over time.

Let's begin.

Come to know the one who
watches the voice, and you will
come to know one of the great
mysteries of creation.

PART 1

AWAKENING CONSCIOUSNESS

IN CASE YOU HAVEN'T NOTICED, you have a mental dialogue going on inside your head that never stops. It just keeps going and going. Have you ever wondered why it talks in there? How does it decide what to say and when to say it? How much of what it says turns out to be true? How much of what it says is even important? And if right now you are hearing, "I don't know what you're talking about. I don't have any voice inside my head!"—that's the voice we're talking about.

Begin the practice of noticing your thoughts.
You are not your thoughts—they are something you're aware of.

When you close your eyes and listen within, what thoughts do you hear? What is it like to be aware that your mind is talking?

THE BEST WAY TO FREE YOURSELF from this incessant chatter is to step back and view it objectively. Just view the voice as a vocalizing mechanism that is capable of making it appear like someone is in there talking to you. Don't think about it; just notice it. No matter what the voice is saying, it's all the same. It doesn't matter if it's saying nice things or mean things, worldly things or spiritual things. It doesn't matter because it's still just a voice talking inside your head.

Close your eyes and say in your mind something that you know is not true, like "My dog is blue." Notice that your mind had no problem saying it. You may not realize it, but your inner voice often says things that aren't true. The mind can (and will) say anything, and it's our responsibility not to believe everything it says.

Write about a time when the voice told you something that turned out not to be true. Can you see that the voice is separate from you and can say anything?

YOU DO HEAR IT when it talks, don't you? Make it say "hello" right now. Say it over and over a few times. Now shout it inside! Can you hear yourself saying "hello" inside? Of course you can. There is a voice talking, and there is you who notices the voice talking. The problem is that it's easy to notice the voice saying "hello," but it's difficult to see that no matter what the voice says, it is still just a voice talking and you listening. There is absolutely nothing that voice can say that is more you than anything else it says.

When you're having a good day, what are a few thoughts you might have about yourself? Write a few sentences describing positive thoughts you are capable of having about yourself.

When you're having a bad day, what are some thoughts you might have about yourself? Write about those thoughts too.

See how vastly different your thoughts about yourself can be. From this perspective, it becomes easier to begin to see that the voice is not you.

THERE IS NOTHING MORE IMPORTANT to true growth than realizing that you are not the voice of the mind—you are the one who hears it. If you don't understand this, you will try to figure out which of the many things the voice says is really you.

Take a few moments to reflect on a time when you had trouble making a decision for or against something. Did you find you were talking to yourself about why you should do this thing, and then later talking to yourself about why you shouldn't? Maybe you even argued with yourself about it. It's like there are multiple people in there wanting different things. But notice that you are aware of all of this. In truth, none of those voices are you; you are the one who is aware of the voices and the indecision.

Write about what it's like to experience the conflicting thoughts of your mind. Then, write about the part of you that notices that this conflict is even going on.

IF YOU WATCH OBJECTIVELY, you will see that when there's a buildup of nervous, fearful, or desire-based energies inside, the voice becomes extremely active. This is easy to see when you are angry with someone and you feel like telling them off. Just watch how many times the inner voice tells them off before you even see them. When energy builds up inside, you want to do something about it. That voice talks because you're not okay inside, and talking releases energy.

Today, notice an exchange that increases your mental agitation. Notice your mind becoming active.

Write about how your mind reacted—the inner dialog that was triggered. Did you begin rehearsing a conversation with someone? Was fear stimulated? Was there a stab of shame, or anger, or need? Can you see that the mind's talk is trying to fix discomfort?

TAKE A MOMENT to examine the difference between your experience of the outside world and your interactions with your inner mental world. You are very accustomed to settling into this playground of the mind and creating and manipulating thoughts.

Observe your surroundings.
Write down what you see outside of yourself.

Now write the
thoughts created by
your mind **about** what
you observe outside of
yourself.

WHAT YOU END UP EXPERIENCING is really a personal presentation of the world according to you, rather than the stark, unfiltered experience of what is really out there. This mental manipulation of the outer experience allows you to buffer reality as it comes in. For example, there are myriad things that you see at any given moment, yet you only narrate a few of them. The ones you discuss in your mind are the ones that matter to you. With this subtle form of preprocessing, you manage to control the experience of reality so that it all fits together inside your mind. Your consciousness is actually experiencing your mental model of reality, not reality itself.

Today, spend time noticing what parts of reality you narrate. Many events go by unnoticed, but what catches your attention and why? When is your narrator most active? What stimulates that inner dialog?

YOU WILL COME TO SEE that the mind talks all the time because you gave it a job to do. You use this mental chatter as a protection mechanism, a form of defense.

Observe the mental chatter designed to solve a particular problem or threat in your life.

What problem is your mind trying to solve? How is your mind trying to solve this problem? What is at stake (what is your mind trying to protect)?

IN THE NAME of attempting to hold the world together, you're really just trying to hold yourself together.

True personal growth is about transcending the part of you that is not okay and needs protection. This is done by constantly remembering that you are the one inside that notices the voice talking. That is the way out. The one inside who is aware that you are always talking to yourself about yourself is always silent. It is a doorway to the depths of your being.

When you awaken in the morning, and when you are going to sleep, notice any chatter you have about keeping situations in control or fixing them. Once you notice, then relax, breathe, and begin to focus on the part of you that is simply aware of the thoughts and feelings you are experiencing.

Write about these thoughts and what it was like to objectively notice them. Was your mind planning? Problem-solving? Worrying? Were you able to observe, relax, breathe, and let the thoughts pass by?

THE BOTTOM LINE IS, you'll never be free of problems until you are free from the part within that has so many problems. When a problem is disturbing you, don't ask, "What should I do about it?" Ask, "What part of me is being disturbed by this?" If you ask, "What should I do about it?" you've already fallen into believing that there really is a problem outside that must be dealt with.

Today, every time something happens that hits your stuff, and you feel your energy changing, ask: "What part of me is being disturbed?" Now contemplate: Is it really the situation that is disturbing you, or are you really disturbing yourself about the situation? Write about what you discover.

29

PROBLEMS ARE GENERALLY NOT what they appear to be. The real problem is that there is something inside of you that can have a problem with almost anything. You have to break the habit of thinking that the solution to your problems is to rearrange things outside. This involves a change from "outer solution consciousness" to "inner solution consciousness." The only permanent solution to your problems is to go inside and let go of the part of you that seems to have so many problems with reality. Once you do that, you'll be clear enough to deal with what's left.

Write a bit about a problem you are having.

Is there something you can let go of inside yourself rather than changing the outside world?

THERE ARE TWO distinct aspects of your inner being. The first is you, the awareness, the witness, the center of your willful intentions; and the other is that which you watch. The problem is, the part that you watch never shuts up. If you could get rid of that part, even for a moment, the peace and serenity would be the nicest vacation you've ever had.

An easy way to see how much the voice talks is to notice when you're taking a shower. Do you just quietly clean your body, or is your mind busy talking? You'll see it keeps talking—maybe it's planning your day, complaining about the bills, or daydreaming about the future. The mind chatters away all the time—in the shower, while you're driving, or while sitting on the bus. But there is a part of you that is simply aware of the chatter. That part, the witness, is always silent. Imagine what it would be like to just peacefully clean your body or sit in your car.

Write about the chatter of your mind that happens in the shower. Is it helpful, bothersome, positive, or negative? How much of it is really necessary?

Now, write about what it would be like to be free from the constant noise caused by your personal thoughts.

YOUR INNER GROWTH IS
COMPLETELY DEPENDENT
UPON THE REALIZATION
THAT THE ONLY WAY
TO FIND PEACE AND
CONTENTMENT IS TO
STOP THINKING
ABOUT YOURSELF.

THERE'S A SEPARATION BETWEEN you and the anger or the jealousy. You are the one who's in there noticing these things. Once you take that seat of consciousness, you can get rid of these personal disturbances. You start by watching. Just be aware that you are aware of what is going on in there. It's easy. What you'll notice is that you're watching a human being's personality with all its strengths and weaknesses. It's as though there's somebody in there with you. You might actually say you have a "roommate."

Contemplate the idea that your own personal thoughts and idiosyncracies are not who you are. Can you see your personality as being a roommate in there with you?

Write about the difference you can see between your seat of awareness and the all too human personality you experience inside (your roommate).

37

THE WAY TO CATCH ON to what your inner roommate is really like is to personify it externally. Make believe that your roommate, the psyche, has a body of its own. You do this by taking the entire personality that you hear talking to you inside and imagine it as a person talking to you on the outside. Just imagine that another person is now saying everything that your inner voice would say. Now spend a day with that person. Just get to know what you live with by letting this voice talk to you.

Take your inner roommate for a walk on your favorite trail or even around the block. Imagine this roommate as your actual companion for the day.

Do you enjoy this person?

What kind of temperament does this person have?

_____

_____

_____

_____

_____

_____

_____

_____

_____

_____

What is it like
to spend a day
with your inner
roommate?

_____

_____

_____

Is this person's
chatter negative,
positive, fearful,
or judgmental?

_____

_____

_____

_____

39

AS IT IS RIGHT NOW, your life is not your own; it belongs to your inner roommate, the psyche. You have to take it back. Stand firm in the seat of the witness and release the hold that the habitual mind has on you. This is your life—reclaim it.

Have you ever had a roommate you had to ask to move out? Negative and noisy thoughts are like a difficult roommate. Today, when these thoughts are stimulated, notice how that affects your energy. Write about that.

Now write about the
new peaceful space you
might create if you asked
this roommate to move
out, or at least stopped
listening to it.

WHO SEES WHEN YOU SEE? Who hears when you hear? Who watches the dreams? Who looks at the image in the mirror?

There is an unchanging observing part of yourself. Take a few deep breaths and connect with this Witness. How does it feel to contact the Witness? Do you feel the peaceful separateness from your mind and outer world?

MAKE BELIEVE that you and I are having a conversation. Typically, in Western cultures, when someone comes up to you and asks, "Excuse me, who are you?" you don't admonish them for asking such a deep question. You tell them your name, for example, Sally Smith. But I'm going to challenge this response by taking out a piece of paper and writing the letters S-a-l-l-y-S-m-i-t-h, and then showing it to you. Is that who you are—a collection of letters? Is that who sees when you see? Obviously not, so you say, "Okay, you're right, I'm sorry. I'm not Sally Smith. That's just a name people call me. It's a label. Really, I'm Frank Smith's wife."

List the things you believe describe who you are. It could include your name, age, gender, occupation, ethnicity, family relationship labels, and so on. Just write down what you'd typically use to answer the question "Who are you?"

Reflect on these labels. Can you see that any of these labels could change, and you would still be in there noticing that they changed? Write about this.

YOU ARE NOT YOUR THOUGHTS. You are simply aware of your thoughts. Finally you say, "Fine, I'm not anything in the outside world and I'm not the emotions. These outer and inner objects come and go and I experience them. Plus, I'm not the thoughts. They can be quiet or noisy, happy or sad. Thoughts are just something else I'm aware of. But who am I?"

Watch your outside environment,
everything you see and hear and feel. What is out there?

_____

_____

_____

_____

_____

_____

_____

Now watch your experience inside (including your mind, your emotions, and the sensations of your body). What do you find in there?

_____

_____

_____

_____

_____

_____

46

As you watched outside and inside, what did you discover about you, the watcher of the inner and outer objects?

IT STARTS TO BECOME A SERIOUS QUESTION:

"Who am I? Who is having all these physical, emotional, and mental experiences?" So you contemplate this question a little deeper. This is done by letting go of the experiences and noticing who is left. You will begin to notice who is experiencing the experience. Eventually, you will get to a point within yourself where you realize that you, the experiencer, have a certain quality. And that quality is awareness, consciousness, an intuitive sense of existence.

Gather three pictures of yourself at different ages. Study these, and reflect:

Who was always in there, no matter what body you had or what clothes you wore? This is your core essence, always present behind the image in the pictures. Write about who you have always been.

THE ESSENCE OF CONSCIOUSNESS is awareness, and awareness has the ability to become more aware of one thing and less aware of something else. In other words, it has the ability to focus itself on certain objects. The teacher says, "Concentrate on what I'm saying." What does that mean? It means focus your consciousness on one place.

Nobody taught you this. It was intuitive and natural. You've always known how to do it.

Focus your attention on an object for two minutes. Observe what happens in your mind and body.

Write about what happened during those two minutes. Were you able to focus without your mind wandering or being distracted by something else? And if your mind wandered, were you able to notice you got distracted, and then refocus on the object?

RIGHT NOW, you are sitting inside the center of consciousness watching your personal TV show. But there are so many interesting objects distracting your consciousness that you can't help but get drawn into them. It's all around you. All of your senses draw you in—sight, sound, taste, smell, and touch—as well as your feelings and your thoughts. But you are really sitting quietly inside looking out at all these objects. Just as the sun does not leave its position in the sky to illuminate objects with its radiating light, so consciousness does not leave its center to project awareness onto the objects of form, thoughts, and emotions. If you ever want to re-center, just start saying "hello" inside, over and over.

Notice the sights, sounds, and smells coming in through your senses. What likes or dislikes arise?

Notice how your mind labels reality according to your personal preferences and frame of reference: "tidy," "messy," "light," "cold," "smells like breakfast cooking."

Now close your eyes and say "hello" over and over to bring you back to your center.

What does it feel like to leave the world of mental labels and return to your center?

WHEN YOU CONTEMPLATE the nature of Self, you are meditating. That is why meditation is the highest state. It is the return to the root of your being, the simple awareness of being aware. Once you become conscious of the consciousness itself, you attain a totally different state. You are now aware of who you are. You have become an awakened being.

Sit for a while with eyes closed, and allow yourself to notice any sensations in your body. Notice any thoughts or emotions that arise, and notice that you are aware of all of this. Then begin to focus back on being aware — can you be simply aware that you are aware?

Write about what it is like to simply notice your thoughts and emotions. What is it like to simply experience the sensations in the body? This is what it feels like to be Awake. Are you beginning to feel the deep presence of awareness in your daily life?

If enjoying a full life means

experiencing high energy, love,

and enthusiasm all the time,

then don't ever close.

PART 2

EXPERIENCING ENERGY

CONSCIOUSNESS is one of the great mysteries in life. Inner energy is another.

The truth is, every movement of your body, every emotion you have, and every thought that passes through your mind is an expenditure of energy.

For example, if you concentrate on a thought and another thought interferes, you will have to assert an opposing force to fight the interfering thought. That requires energy, and it can wear you out.

Observe the competing thoughts in your mind— the "what ifs," the "buts," or the "shoulds" that compete for your attention. Write about how different thoughts affect your energy.

CREATING THOUGHTS, holding onto thoughts, recalling thoughts, generating emotions, controlling emotions, and disciplining powerful inner drives, all require a tremendous expenditure of energy. Where does all this energy come from? Why is the energy there sometimes, and at other times you feel completely drained? Have you ever noticed that when you are mentally and emotionally drained, food doesn't help that much? Conversely, if you look at the times in your life when you were in love, or excited and inspired by something, you were so filled with energy that you didn't even want to eat. This energy we are discussing does not come from the calories your body burns from food. There is a source of energy you can draw upon from inside. It is distinct from the outer energy source.

Think about a time when you felt tired and drained, regardless of what you ate or how well you slept. Perhaps it happened around a breakup or other personal loss. Perhaps there was something you tried but failed to achieve.

Now recollect: what happened that caused the inner energy to start flowing well again? Did an event occur that you liked? Did you get inspired by a new project?

As you reflect on this ebb and flow, what do you notice? What causes your inner energy flow to diminish, and what causes it to replenish?

YOU'LL SEE, if you watch carefully...that you have a phenomenal amount of energy inside of you. It doesn't come from food and it doesn't come from sleep. This energy is always available to you. At any moment you can draw upon it. It just wells up and fills you from inside. When you're filled with this energy, you feel like you could take on the world. When it is flowing strongly, you can actually feel it coursing through you in waves. It gushes up spontaneously from deep inside and restores, replenishes, and recharges you.

Remember a time you felt your energy awakened, regardless of how much you had slept or what you had eaten. A time when the energy seemed to come from a greater source that surged through you, giving you stamina and joy.

Write about this experience with upwelling energy. What was the context (where, who, when, what)? What was it like to feel this?

THE ONLY REASON you don't feel this energy all the time is because you block it. You block it by closing your heart, by closing your mind, and by pulling yourself into a restrictive space inside. This closes you off from all the energy. When you close your heart or close your mind, you hide in the darkness within you. There is no light. There is no energy. There is nothing flowing. The energy is still there but it can't get in. That is what it means to be "blocked."

Ask yourself, "Why do I close?" Now ask, "Is it really worth it?"

Write about how it feels to be shut down.

How does it affect your mind and heart? How does it affect your energy flow?

How does it affect your view of the world around you?

65

ALTHOUGH VARIOUS ENERGY CENTERS exist within you, the one you intuitively know the most about opening and closing is your heart. Let's say that you love somebody, and you feel very open in their presence. Because you trust them, your walls come down allowing you to feel lots of high energy. But if they do something you don't like, the next time you see them you don't feel so high. You don't feel as much love. Instead, you feel a tightness in your chest. This happens because you closed your heart. The heart is an energy center, and it can open or close. The yogis call energy centers chakras. When you close your heart center, energy can't flow in. When energy can't flow in, there's darkness. Depending upon how closed you are, you either feel tremendous disturbance or overwhelming lethargy. Often people fluctuate between these two states.

Think about a time someone you loved acted in a way that hurt you. Did you feel your heart close? Did it actually hurt and get tight in the middle of your chest? Write down the thoughts that began passing through your mind. Be sure to include the ways you were trying to "solve" the situation.

Write about what it would be like to be able to watch all of this from a state of clear awareness. Can you describe a really clear way to deal with this situation as opposed to your traditional reaction?

IF YOU LIKE ENERGY, and you do, then don't ever close. The more you learn to stay open, the more the energy can flow into you. You practice opening by not closing. Any time you start to close, ask yourself whether you really want to cut off the energy flow. Because if you want, you can learn to stay open no matter what happens in this world. You just make a commitment to explore your capacity for receiving unlimited energy. You simply decide not to close.

Think about a specific time when you stayed open even when circumstances or internal urges prompted you to close. Was it a struggle? Write about why you decided to put out the effort not to close.

Complete this statement: "I can stay open to my deepest source of energy, no matter the circumstance, by

_____."

IF YOU REALLY WANT TO STAY OPEN, pay attention when you feel love and enthusiasm. Then ask yourself why you can't feel this all the time. Why does it have to go away? The answer is obvious: it only goes away if you choose to close. By closing, you are actually making the choice not to feel openness and love. You throw love away all the time. You feel love until somebody says something you don't like, and then you give up the love. You feel enthused about your job until someone criticizes something, and then you want to quit. It's your choice. You can either close because you don't like what happened, or you can keep feeling love and enthusiasm by not closing.

Practice not throwing away love. During a time when you feel open, pay attention to what causes you to close up again. Maybe something happened that you didn't like. Whatever you experienced, write it down.

Write about how it affects you when you hold onto reactive disturbances as real.

_____

_____

_____

_____

_____

_____

_____

_____

_____

_____

_____

How would it be if you chose to not let your reactions bother you?

When you notice you're reacting to an event you don't like, ask yourself, "Is this worth closing over?"

THROUGH MEDITATION, through awareness and willful efforts, you can learn to keep your centers open. You do this by just relaxing and releasing. You do this by not buying into the concept that there is anything worth closing over. Remember, if you love life, nothing is worth closing over. Nothing, ever, is worth closing your heart over.

Call to mind a situation that is agitating you. Write about the feelings of agitation and the thoughts that come with that situation.

These feelings and thoughts are your cue to relax and release. Now write about how you might consciously choose to stay open. What is it like to relax and release in the midst of disturbance and reactivity? Do you come back to a feeling of openness sooner than if you had closed up?

IF AT ANY GIVEN POINT in time the heart happens to open, we fall in love. If at any given point in time it happens to close, the love stops. If the heart happens to hurt, we get angry, and if we stop feeling it altogether, we get empty. All of these different things happen because the heart goes through changes. These energy shifts and variations that take place in the heart run your life.

In truth, you are not your heart. You are the experiencer of your heart. Today, notice how you experience your heart, including all the positive and negative emotions. Do you find that you identify very closely with your heart? Do the feelings in your heart drive your thoughts and actions?

_____

_____

_____

_____

_____

_____

_____

_____

_____

_____

_____

_____

74

Practice noticing, and as you practice, write about how you experience your heart energy Can you experience the heart energy, and all its shifts and changes, without identifying with it and letting it dictate your actions?

THE HEART is actually very simple to understand. It is an energy center, a chakra. It is one of the most beautiful and powerful energy centers, and one that affects our daily lives. As we have seen, an energy center is an area within your being through which your energy focuses, distributes, and flows. This energy flow has been referred to as Shakti, Spirit, and Chi, and it plays an intricate part in your life. You feel the heart's energy all the time. Think about what it is like to feel love in your heart. Think about what it is like to feel inspiration and enthusiasm pour from your heart. Think about what it is like to feel energy well up in your heart making you confident and strong.

Meditate on your heart chakra: close your eyes and breathe into your heart, right in the center of your chest. Feel your heart expand with each breath. What does it feel like when you are just meditating on your heart, and nothing in particular is happening to make it open or close?

_____

_____

_____

_____

_____

_____

_____

_____

Now, as you go about your day, notice when you feel the heart open and close.

Write about what feelings you have.
For example, when the heart is open,
do you feel inspired, passionate, grateful,
free? Whatever your feelings, notice them
as they arise and pass. Are you capable
of experiencing all the feelings that move
through your heart? Or do you resist
some feelings and cling to others?

MOMENT AFTER MOMENT, experiences are coming in and you're learning and growing. Your heart and mind are expanding, and you are being touched at a very deep level. If experience is the best teacher, there's nothing that comes close to the experience of life.

What it means to live life is to experience the moment that is passing through you, and then experience the next moment, and then the next. Many different experiences will come in and pass through you. It's a phenomenal system when it is working properly. If you could live in that state, you would be a fully aware being. That is how an awakened being lives in the "now." They are present, life is present, and the wholeness of life is passing through them. Imagine if you were so fully present during each experience of life that it was touching you to the depth of your being. Every moment would be a stimulating, moving experience because you would be completely open, and life would be flowing right through you.

Everyone has had experiences in their life that have touched them deeply and fully. Take a moment and recall a time when you felt completely fulfilled. Maybe you were driving, turned down a road, and faced an exquisite sunset—with beautiful orange and magentas. It was the most beautiful thing you'd ever seen, and it filled you with a sense of awe, appreciation, and contentment. Every moment can touch you that deeply.

Write about what it would be like if every moment touched you to the depth of your being. It blows your mind that your lungs breathe, that you can walk, that a bird can sing, and that a mean person can yell at you. Can you let every moment touch your soul?

YOU CAN HEAR AN INSTRUMENT,

BUT YOU FEEL YOUR HEART.

AND IF YOU THINK THAT YOU

FEEL AN INSTRUMENT, IT'S

ONLY BECAUSE IT TOUCHED

YOUR HEART. YOUR HEART

IS AN INSTRUMENT MADE OF

EXTREMELY SUBTLE ENERGY

THAT FEW PEOPLE COME

TO APPRECIATE.

A SAMSKARA IS A BLOCKAGE, an event that got stuck. All the subsequent experiences are trying to pass through you, but something has happened inside that has left this past experience unfinished. Life must now compete with this blocked event for your attention, and the impression does not just sit in there quietly. You will see that your tendency is to think about it constantly. This is all in an attempt to find a way to process it through your mind. Because you resisted, it got stuck, and now you have a problem. You see the thoughts start up. Thought after thought goes on inside. It drives you crazy in there. All that inner noise is just your attempt to process the blocked energy and get it out of the way.

How does resistance show up for you? Is it tension in the body? Or negative thoughts? Notice your mind react. Notice the thoughts that follow.

Notice what you do in response to those thoughts. What actions follow when you resist and the energy gets trapped? Maybe you'll feel like having a few extra glasses of wine, or an extra bowl of ice cream, or staying up late to watch shows. Maybe you'll actually end up saying something you had decided not to say.

Write about the sequence of feelings, thoughts and actions that happen when you get stuck.

IN THE YOGIC TRADITION, an unfinished energy pattern is called a samskara. This is a Sanskrit word meaning "impression," and in the yogic teachings it is considered one of the most important influences affecting your life. A samskara is a blockage, an impression from the past. It's an unfinished energy pattern that ends up running your life.

What are some of the unfinished energy patterns within you? It's actually very easy to find them—just start noticing what typically triggers your emotional reactions throughout your day. Does it hit you deeply when you feel you're not receiving attention and affection? Do you find yourself getting defensive when you're criticized? Can you trace these sensitivities back to earlier experiences in your life? Just notice and write about your experiences that point to the impressions deep within.

TWO KINDS OF EXPERIENCES can occur that block the heart. You are either trying to push energies away because they bother you, or you are trying to keep energies close because you like them. In both cases, you are not letting them pass, and you are wasting precious energy by blocking the flow through resisting and clinging.

We've all had experiences that we've resisted or tried to keep within ourselves. Maybe you got embarrassed while giving a speech in grade school, and now you get nervous every time you have to speak publicly. Or perhaps you got the lead role in your high school drama team's yearly play, and you still tell everyone about it and pine to be a great actor.

Write about a time when you had an experience that was not comfortable, and you pushed it away.

Does it still try to come up? Do you still find yourself continuing to resist it?

How does it feel to cling to something that is no longer happening?

Now, write about an experience you enjoyed so much that you didn't want it to stop.

...UNENDING INSPIRATION, UNENDING LOVE, AND UNENDING OPENNESS—That is the natural state of a healthy heart.

To achieve this state, simply allow the experiences of life to come in and pass through your being. If old energies come back up because you were unable to process them before, let go of them now.

Set your intention to let the experiences of life unfold rather than allowing old blocked energy to create resistance. Write about a situation or event that triggered you today. Maybe you were holding onto a past fear or concern that was stimulated by the current situation.

Were you able to intentionally notice the blocked energy, or inner disturbance, and then release it? What energy did you experience and how did you notice and release? What did it feel like to not resist the situation and your reactions?

OF COURSE IT HURTS when it comes up. It was stored with pain; it's going to release with pain. You have to decide if you want to continue to walk around with stored pain blocking your heart and limiting your life. The alternative is to be willing to let it go when it gets stimulated. It only hurts for a minute and then it's over.

Write about what it feels like to have stored pain from the past start to resurface in your heart.

Write about what you usually do to avoid or minimize the uncomfortable experience. Do you have habitual activities you use to avoid having to feel the pain resurface?

Imagine what it would be like to let go and be free from the stored pain running your life.

YOUR REWARD IS a permanently open heart. There is no more valve. You live in love, and it feeds you and strengthens you. That is an open heart. That is the instrument of the heart as it was meant to be. Allow yourself to experience every note the heart can play. If you relax and release, this purification of your heart is a wonderful thing. Set your eyes on the highest state you can imagine and don't take them off. If you slip, just get back up. It doesn't matter. The very fact that you even want to go through this process of freeing the energy flow means you are great. You will get there. Just keep letting go.

Write about how, today, you experienced every note your heart can play. It can be anything—how you enjoyed the sunshine, and how you felt an annoyance, and then let it pass through. Write about how full and rich your life will be as you free your inner energy.

...IT IS NOT DIFFICULT TO SEE that the most primal energy flow is the survival instinct. During eons of evolution, from the simplest of living forms to the most complex, there has always been the day-to-day struggle to protect oneself. In our highly evolved cooperative social structures, this survival instinct has gone through evolutionary changes. Many of us no longer lack food, water, clothing, or shelter; nor do we regularly face life-threatening physical danger. As a result, the protective energies have adapted toward defending the individual psychologically, rather than physiologically. We now experience the daily need to defend our self-concepts rather than our bodies. Our major struggles end up being with our own inner fears, insecurities, and destructive behavior patterns, and not with outside forces.

What self-concepts do you feel the need to defend, protect, and preserve? Perhaps you need to be seen as smart or successful; desirable or attractive; strong or stoic? What threatens these self-concepts? What happens when your self-concepts are challenged— do you immediately defend? Do you feel fear? Write freely and honestly, staying open to whatever comes up.

YOU KNOW EXACTLY how to close your heart and put up a psychological protective shield. You know exactly how to close down the centers to avoid being too receptive and sensitive to the different energies coming in and causing fear.

When you close down and protect yourself, you are pulling a shell around the part of you that is weak. This is the part that feels it needs protection even though no physical attack is taking place.
You are protecting your ego, your self-concept.

Today, just notice when you react defensively to something.
Remember that you are able to observe this happening;
you can witness yourself in reaction mode.

Now reflect on the day. What happened? What felt sensitive? Did you feel your heart center tighten up? What thoughts did you have about the situation, and did you say anything to defend yourself? What were you protecting?

YOU WILL GET TO A POINT in your growth where you understand that if you protect yourself, you will never be free. It's that simple. Because you're scared, you have locked yourself within your house and pulled down all the shades. Now it's dark and you want to feel the sunlight, but you can't. It's impossible. If you close and protect yourself, you are locking this scared, insecure person within your heart. You will never be free that way.

The easiest way to open is to cease to protect yourself. Try an experiment today. See if you can go through an entire day without saying or doing anything to defend yourself or prove yourself.
This will require that you be ultra-aware of the energy that is motivating your words and actions.

When the day is over, write about what happened.

_____

_____

_____

_____

_____

_____

_____

_____

_____

_____

Did you notice how many of your thoughts and actions are driven by the desire to defend or prove? When you chose not to act from that place, did you feel vulnerable and exposed? Did you feel peaceful? Do you see the potential of being free from the constricted energy of fear and protection? What would that be like?

CONSCIOUSNESS HAS THE TENDENCY

to focus on disturbance, and disturbed energies inside are no exception. These disturbed energies will draw your consciousness to them. But you do not have to let this happen. You really do have the ability to disengage and fall back behind them.

When the energies inside start to move, you do not have to
go there. For instance, when your thoughts start,
you do not have to go with them.
If you want to be free, then every time you feel any change
in the energy flow, relax behind it. Don't fight with it, don't try
to change it, and don't judge it.

Our thoughts are often driven by the disturbed energy inside us.
Today, watch for such thoughts entering your mind (for example,
"I wish I'd done _____yesterday!" or,
"Why did _____ say that to me at work?").
Notice the thought arise and any energetic disturbance
you feel in your heart. Now breathe, relax, and
watch the thoughts and disturbance move through.

_____

_____

_____

_____

_____

If you relax
behind the thoughts and
inner disturbances that bother
you, what happens? Are you able
to be okay with the disturbed
thoughts and feelings? Can
you see that disturbance is just
energy, and it can't hurt you?
When you are no longer
afraid of inner disturbance,
you will be free of it.

EVENTUALLY, what started as a passing thought or emotion can become the center of your entire life. If you don't let go, it can get completely out of control.

A wise person remains centered enough to let go every time the energy shifts into a defensive mode. The moment the energy moves and you feel your consciousness start to get drawn into it, you relax and release. Letting go means falling behind the energy instead of going into it.

Today, try to notice when your energy shifts into defensive mode. How does your body respond to the shift? For example, do you feel tightness in your shoulders, or a pain in your belly?

How do your thoughts change? Notice what thoughts show up.

When these defenses are triggered, practice coming back to your centered self by relaxing and releasing. Write about this experience of noticing, relaxing, and recentering, including what felt effective and what felt challenging.

SCIENCE HAS SHOWN
US HOW AN UNDERLYING
ENERGY FIELD FORMS INTO
ATOMS, WHICH THEN BIND
TOGETHER INTO MOLECULES,
AND ULTIMATELY MANIFEST
INTO THE ENTIRE PHYSICAL
UNIVERSE. THE SAME IS
TRUE INSIDE OF US.

WE TEND TO LET OURSELVES get bothered by the little, meaningless things that happen every day. For example, somebody beeps at you at the stoplight. As these little things happen, you will feel your energy change. The moment you feel a change, relax your shoulders and relax the area around your heart. The moment the energy moves, you simply relax and release. Play with letting go and falling behind this sense of being bothered.

Today, when you notice yourself getting disturbed by something, practice relaxing very deeply in the midst of the disturbance. Can you, the consciousness, relax even if the negative thoughts and disturbance continue? It will feel as though the disturbance is out in front of you, and you are falling back behind it.

What does it feel like to fall behind the disturbance?

Write about this experience of noticing disturbance, relaxing and releasing, and allowing the disturbance to pass through.

THERE'S A PLACE DEEP INSIDE of you where the consciousness touches the energy, and the energy touches the consciousness. That's where your work is. From that place, you let go. Once you've let go, every minute of every day, year after year, then that's where you'll live. Nothing will be able to take your seat of consciousness from you. You'll learn to stay there. After you've put years and years into this process and learned to let go no matter how deep the pain, you will achieve a great state. You will break the ultimate habit: the constant draw of the lower self. You will then be free to explore the nature and source of your true being—Pure Consciousness.

The passages in this section of the journal have explored ways to become more aware of the place within you where consciousness and energy meet. Having worked through this section, how do you now recognize the draw of the lower self within yourself? Reflect on the thoughts, feelings, bodily sensations, and other cues you've noticed when disturbances or blockages arise.

Write about what you've learned about letting go of these disturbances.

Change can be viewed as

either exciting or frightening,

but regardless of how we view

it, we must all face the fact

that change is the very

nature of life.

PART 3

FREEING
YOURSELF

THE EXPLORATION OF SELF is inextricably interwoven with the unfolding of one's life. The natural ups and downs of life can either generate personal growth or create personal fears. Which of these dominates is completely dependent upon how we view change. Change can be viewed as either exciting or frightening, but regardless of how we view it, we must all face the fact that change is the very nature of life. If you have a lot of fear, you won't like change. You'll try to create a world around you that is predictable, controllable, and definable. You'll try to create a world that doesn't stimulate your fears. Fear doesn't want to feel itself; it's actually afraid of itself. So you utilize the mind in an attempt to manipulate life for the purpose of not feeling fear.

Write about a change that is happening in your life—large or small—that is bringing up resistance or concerns. What are your thoughts saying about this change? Are you trying to keep it from happening, or are you trying to convince yourself that everything is going to be fine? What would happen if you allowed yourself to feel the discomfort that comes with change before you decided how to deal with it?

PEOPLE DON'T UNDERSTAND that fear is a thing. It's just another object in the universe that you are capable of experiencing. You can do one of two things with fear: you can recognize that you have it and work to release it, or you can keep it and try to hide from it.

We all have fears inside that we keep actively avoiding. Pay attention to a current fear that's causing you trouble. Or, recall a habitual longtime fear that continues to cause you disturbance.

Write about what you typically do to avoid feeling these fears. What techniques have you used to avoid fear, and how well do they really work? Does the fear go away for good, or just temporarily?

Now, write about what it is like to work through a fear, instead of avoiding it. What techniques have you used to work through the fear and release it? How well do they work?

AS YOU GROW SPIRITUALLY, you will realize that your attempts to protect yourself from your problems actually create more problems. If you attempt to arrange people, places, and things so they don't disturb you, it will begin to feel like life is against you. You'll feel that life is a struggle and that every day is heavy because you have to control and fight with everything. There will be competition, jealousy, and fear. You will feel that anyone, at any moment, could cause you disturbance.

Today, notice when the dialog in your mind turns to how to make sure certain things happen, or how to keep certain things from happening. Write about what you noticed about these anxious thoughts.

_____

_____

_____

_____

_____

_____

_____

_____

_____

Next, write about any thoughts that arose about making the anxious thoughts stop.

_____

_____

_____

_____

Notice how avoiding a problem puts you into an endless loop of thoughts and plans to keep from having to deal with the disturbance. In each case your mind keeps trying to label and control your disturbance, whether it is the fear itself or the anxiety that arises from resisting the fear. What would it be like, in such a moment, to let go of control and just watch the disturbance play out inside? Try this, and write about what you discover.

IF YOU SIT WITHIN THE SELF,
YOU WILL EXPERIENCE THE
STRENGTH OF YOUR INNER BEING
EVEN WHEN YOUR HEART FEELS
WEAK. THIS IS THE ESSENCE OF
THE PATH. THIS IS THE ESSENCE
OF A SPIRITUAL LIFE. ONCE YOU
LEARN THAT IT'S OKAY TO FEEL
INNER DISTURBANCES, AND THAT
THEY CAN NO LONGER DISTURB
YOUR SEAT OF CONSCIOUSNESS,
YOU WILL BE FREE.

THE ALTERNATIVE IS to decide not to fight with life. You realize and accept that life is not under your control. Life is continuously changing, and if you're trying to control it, you'll never be able to fully live it. Instead of living life, you'll be afraid of life.

Today choose not to fight with life as it's happening. Then notice that an event happens that triggers fear in you. It will feel like that event is out of your control, and you'll want to control it. Notice what it's like inside when the fear is being triggered. Is there mental chatter? Do you feel the pull and churn of blocked energy in your body?

Now, tell yourself that it is okay to feel fear, and you don't have to do anything about it. What changes?

Write about what it was like when the fear was triggered, and what it was like when you let fear exist and went about your life.

THAT WHICH IS BLOCKED and buried within you forms the root of fear. Fear is caused by blockages in the flow of your energy. When your energy is blocked, it can't come up and feed your heart. Therefore, your heart becomes weak. When your heart is weak it becomes susceptible to lower vibrations, and one of the lowest of all vibrations is fear.

What is one fear, or fear-driven emotion (such as anger, envy, or jealousy), you find yourself experiencing?

Write about the experience that bothered you in the past and caused the blockage that is now manifesting as this fear.

THE PURPOSE OF SPIRITUAL EVOLUTION is to remove the blockages that cause your fear. The alternative is to protect your blockages so that you don't have to feel fear. To do this, however, you will have to try to control everything in order to avoid your inner issues. It's hard to understand how we decided that avoiding our inner issues is an intelligent thing to do, but everybody's doing it. Everyone is saying, "I will do every single thing I can to keep my stuff. If you say anything that disturbs me, I will defend myself. I'll yell at you and make you take it back. If you cause any disturbance inside of me, I will make you so sorry." In other words, if somebody does something that stimulates fear, you think they did something wrong. You then do everything you can to make sure they never do it again. First you defend yourself, and then you protect yourself. You do whatever you can to keep from feeling disturbance.

Identify an issue stimulating some difficult emotions. Describe what you perceive as the "offense": the thoughts you have about who did what, when, and how.

_____

_____

_____

_____

_____

_____

_____

_____

_____

Now, write about the issue from a different perspective. Ask yourself, "Why am I being bothered by this?" Is there a blockage of fear, shame, or perhaps an old sadness that is being triggered? Notice the Self who can observe the difficult emotions.

_____

_____

_____

_____

_____

_____

_____ Now, move back into

_____ the seat of the witness

_____ to observe the pain

_____ and the tendency to do

_____ something about it. Can

_____ you withstand the need to

_____ protect yourself, and then

_____ let the blockage go?

_____

_____

_____

EVENTUALLY, YOU BECOME wise enough to realize that you do not want that stuff inside of you. It doesn't matter who stimulates it. It doesn't matter what situation hits it. It doesn't matter whether it makes sense, or whether it seems fair or not. Unfortunately, most of us are not that wise. We're really not trying to be free of our stuff; we're trying to justify keeping it.

Does clinging to the drama of your stored stuff make you happy?
What would it look like to not have this stuff impacting your life.
How might you feel differently?
What might you do differently? Write about this.

IF YOU TRULY WANT TO GROW SPIRITUALLY, you'll realize that keeping your stuff is keeping you trapped. Eventually you'll want out, at any cost. You will then realize that life is actually trying to help you. Life is surrounding you with people and situations that stimulate growth. You don't have to decide who's right or wrong. You don't have to worry about other people's issues. You only have to be willing to open your heart in the face of anything and everything, and permit the purification process to take place.

What are you facing right now that feels difficult? What is it teaching you about the stuff being triggered within you? Where is the opportunity for growth—that is, where is life giving you an opening to witness and move beyond your personal blockages?

THE STUFF THAT HOLDS YOU DOWN periodically rears its head. When it does, let it go. You simply permit the pain to come up into your heart and pass through. If you do that, it will pass. If you are sincerely seeking truth, you'll let go every time. This is the beginning and end of the entire path—you surrender yourself to the process of emptying yourself. When you work with this, you start to learn the subtler laws of the process of letting go.

Every time you let go, there is less stuff inside of you.
It may not all pass through at once, but if you keep practicing,
over time, the blockages will release.
Today, when your stuff comes up, practice letting go in the moment:
observe the pain, allow it to be, and let it pass through.
Choose an approach to letting go that works for you—perhaps practicing
either acceptance or compassion in the moment of disturbance.

At the end of the day, write about your experience. What blocked energy did you surrender?

How did you let it go? Were you able, in the moment, to see the experience as an opportunity for growth?

FIRST, YOU MUST BE AWARE that there is something within you that needs to be released. You must then be aware that you, the one who notices the stuff coming up, are distinct from what you're experiencing. You are noticing it, but who are you? This place of centered awareness is the seat of the witness, the seat of Self.

When your heart gets hit, notice the disturbance happening, allow yourself to be aware that you feel hurt, and then ask yourself, "Who notices this?" Don't answer the question, just feel the answer within yourself.

What is it like to be the one who experiences disturbance—instead of being the one who is disturbed?

IF YOU DON'T LET GO, you'll notice that the energy that got stimulated in your heart works like a magnet. It's a phenomenally attractive force that will pull your consciousness into it. The next thing you know, you won't be there. You won't maintain the same perspective of awareness that you had when you first noticed the disturbance. You will leave the seat of objective awareness from which you saw your heart begin to react, and you will get involved in the shifting energies coming from your heart. Some time later you'll come back and realize you weren't there. You'll come back and realize that you were totally lost in your stuff. Then you will hope that you didn't say or do anything you'll regret.

Remember the last time you experienced a disturbance or discomfort. How long were you lost in your stuff? When did you first notice you had gotten lost? When you woke back up and recentered yourself, was it a struggle? In hindsight, could you have done better with letting go when the disturbance originally came up?

CONSCIOUSNESS IS ALWAYS drawn to the most distracting object: the bumped toe, the loud noise, or the hurting heart. It's the same law, both inside and out. The consciousness goes to the place that distracts it the most. That's what we mean when we say, "It was so loud it caught my attention." It drew your consciousness to it. When a blockage gets hit, this same attraction takes place, and the consciousness gets pulled to the source of discomfort.

The next time your attention is drawn to an inner disturbance, observe this discomfort. What types of thoughts are created? What happens to your energy?

Now shift back into the seat of awareness and observe what is going on outside of you, instead of inside. What can you focus on outside so that you aren't so fixated on your inner disturbance?

From your seat of awareness,
you have the choice to focus on whatever objects
you choose, outside or inside. Next time you get
disturbed inside, experiment with this.

ONCE ACTIVATED, the blockage must run its course. If you don't let go, you get sucked in. You are no longer free; you are caught. Once you fall from your seat of relative clarity, you are under the mercy of the disturbed energy. This is the anatomy of falling. When you're in this state of disturbance, your tendency will be to act in order to try to fix things.

When was the last time you got truly lost in a state of disturbance? What kinds of things did you say or do?

Afterward, how did you feel about how you spoke to your friends or family or coworkers? Would you wish to act differently next time, knowing that if you don't let go the disturbance must run its course?

DON'T FALL. LET GO. No matter what it is, let it go. The bigger it is, the higher the reward of letting go and the worse the fall if you don't. It's pretty black-and-white. You either let go or you don't. There really isn't anything in between. So let all of your blockages and disturbances become the fuel for the journey. That which is holding you down can become a powerful force that raises you up. You just have to be willing to take the ascent.

As soon as your center of awareness starts getting drawn into negative energy, notice that it's happening. Negative thoughts or a focus on what you dislike—these are clues that your center of awareness is shifting. Did you feel like quitting your job, or hanging up on your spouse, or slamming a door? All these are reminders to let go.

Write about how you noticed the magnetic pull of disturbances and whether you were able to catch it happening.

Were you able to let go? Did it happen quickly or slowly, partially or fully?

ULTIMATELY, if there is something disturbing inside of you, you have to make a choice. You can compensate for the disturbance by going outside in an attempt to avoid feeling it, or you can simply remove the thorn and not focus your life around it.

Do not doubt your ability to remove the root cause of the disturbance inside of you. It really can go away. You can look deep within yourself, to the core of your being, and decide that you don't want the weakest part of you running your life. You want to be free of this. You want to talk to people because you find them interesting, not because you're lonely. You want to have relationships with people because you genuinely like them, not because you need for them to like you. You want to love because you truly love, not because you need to avoid your inner problems. How do you free yourself? In the deepest sense, you free yourself by finding yourself.

Spend a few minutes acknowledging the inner thorn with which you are struggling. Notice the thoughts that are associated with this thorn ("I can't believe I actually said that. It was so stupid. After all this time, I'm still embarrassed to ever see those people again."). Notice the way your body responds to the thoughts. Do you feel tension? Do you feel a dropping sensation in your heart? Inhale and exhale for five deep breaths as you notice these thoughts and sensations happening. This inner disturbance is not who you are, and it does not have to run your life.

Now, reflect and write.
Ask: Who sees this?
Who watches the emotions?
Do you see the potential for
freeing yourself by no longer
identifying with the thorns?

THE PREREQUISITE TO TRUE FREEDOM IS TO DECIDE THAT YOU DO NOT WANT TO SUFFER ANYMORE. YOU MUST DECIDE THAT YOU WANT TO ENJOY YOUR LIFE AND THAT THERE IS NO REASON FOR STRESS, INNER PAIN, OR FEAR.

IF YOU WANT, you can simply permit the disturbances to come up, and you can let them go. Since your inner thorns are simply blocked energies from the past, they can be released. The problem is, you either completely avoid situations that would cause them to release, or you push them back down in the name of protecting yourself.

Today, experiment with letting a disturbance rise. What are your first reactions as it rises? Do you race to avoid it somehow? Instead, allow yourself to observe and make room for the disturbance.

Write about what happens when you release it. What do you feel about the overall experience?

A FEELING OF EMPTINESS is an object; it is something you feel. But who feels it? Your way out is just to notice who's noticing.

What can you do to solve this feeling of emptiness besides eating something, calling somebody, or doing something else that might quiet it down? What you can do is notice that you noticed.

When you allow disturbances to rise; what inner pain arises? Perhaps it is loneliness, or shame, or worry.

When you see this pain,
ask yourself, "Who notices this?"
Relax back into the place from which
you notice. Write about what it is like to
notice that you noticed the pain. Were
you able to rest back into the part of
you that notices? The one who
notices is completely
free of pain.

THE ONE WHO NOTICES is already free. If you want to be free of these energies, you must allow them to pass through you instead of hiding them inside of you.

Ever since you were a child, you've had energies going on inside. Wake up and realize that you are in there, and you have a sensitive person in there with you. Simply watch that sensitive part of you feel disturbance. See it feel jealousy, need, and fear. These feelings are just part of the nature of a human being. If you pay attention, you will see that they are not you; they are just something you're feeling and experiencing. You are the indwelling being that is aware of all of this. If you maintain your center, you can learn to appreciate and respect even the difficult experiences.

Do you notice there's a sensitive person in there with you? You can stay in the seat of awareness and compassionately raise that part of you. Practice letting the sensitivities and feelings exist. Then gently work on letting go of that part of you, with the understanding that this person with all their sensitivities is just something you are aware of. When you let go of the lower self, all of its energies are integrated into your true being.

Write about how you can let these sensitivities pass through. Respect them, love them, and let them go. What does it feel like to let them pass and to no longer identify with them?

YOU CAN EXPERIENCE these very human states without getting lost in them or resisting them. You can notice that you notice and just watch how experiencing loneliness affects you. Does your posture change? Do you breathe slower or faster? What goes on when loneliness is given the space it needs to pass through you? Be an explorer. Witness it, and then it will go. If you don't get absorbed in it, the experience will soon pass and something else will come up. Just enjoy all of it. If you can do this, you will be free, and a world of pure energy will open up within you.

Today, witness your thorns (samskaras) when they are hit. Can you simply experience your reactions with openness and compassion. Explore allowing and accepting the thorn. Write about the experience.

153

THE MORE YOU SIT IN THE SELF,

the more you will begin to feel an energy that you have never experienced before. It comes up from behind, rather than in front where you experience your mind and emotions. When you are no longer absorbed in your melodrama but, instead, sit comfortably deep inside the seat of awareness, you will start to feel this flow of energy coming up from deep within. This flow has been called Shakti. This flow has been called Spirit. This is what you begin to experience if you hang out with the Self instead of hanging out with inner disturbances. You don't have to get rid of loneliness; you just cease to be involved with it. It's just another thing in the universe, like cars, grass, and the stars. It's none of your business. Just let things go. That's what the Self does.

Recall a time when you felt rushes of high energy inside of you. Maybe it happened when you had your first child or when you got the attention of someone you admire. Under what circumstances does the high energy come up for you? How is your experience of that energy flow different from how you experience your mind and emotions? What words would you use to describe that energy?

_____

_____

_____

_____

_____

_____

IF YOU SIT WITHIN THE SELF, you will experience the strength of your inner being even when your heart feels weak. This is the essence of the path. This is the essence of a spiritual life. Once you learn that it's okay to feel inner disturbances, and that they can no longer disturb your seat of consciousness, you will be free. You will begin to be sustained by the inner energy flow that comes from behind you. When you have tasted the ecstasy of the inner flow, you can walk in this world and the world will never touch you. That's how you become a free being— you transcend.

Reflect on how you can walk through life, every day, allowing disturbance to come up and pass. How does it feel to know that you are allowed to simply let it go?

Write about what it is like to be at peace with the experience of disturbance. Can you see the potential to live in a deeper energy flow that is independent of the shallow waters of personal disturbance?

EVERY DAY WE BEAR A BURDEN that we should not be bearing. We fear that we are not good enough or that we will fail. We experience insecurity, anxiety, and self-consciousness. We fear that people will turn on us, take advantage of us, or stop loving us. All of these things burden us tremendously. As we try to have open and loving relationships, and as we try to succeed and express ourselves, there is an inner weight that we carry. This weight is the fear of experiencing pain, anguish, or sorrow. Every day we are either feeling it, or we are protecting ourselves from feeling it. It is such a core influence that we don't even realize how prevalent it is.

Can you see how prevalent the underlying fear of rejection and failure is within you? Write about some of the ways that you try to avoid experiencing this.

Now, express what it would be like to replace these underlying fears with love, excitement, and inspiration as the motivation for all your actions.

YOU THINK ABOUT your psychological well-being all the time. People are constantly thinking things like, "What if I get put on the spot? What should I say? I get so nervous if I'm not prepared." That is suffering. That constant, anxious inner talk is a form of suffering: "Can I really trust him? What if I expose myself and I get taken advantage of? I don't ever want to go through that again." That is the pain of having to think about yourself all the time.

Have you noticed how many personal thoughts are going on all the time? The next time you notice all these personal and fearful thoughts, pause for a moment. Ask yourself if you want to be that person or do you want to be free.

Write about what happens when you step back and decide not to get involved in your personal melodrama. Can you see that you are separate from these thoughts, and they are not you?

_____

_____

_____

_____

_____

_____

_____

_____

_____

_____

_____

IF YOU MISTREAT an animal, it becomes afraid. This is what has happened to your psyche. You have mistreated it by giving it a responsibility that is incomprehensible. Just stop for a moment and see what you have given your mind to do. You said to your mind, "I want everyone to like me. I don't want anyone to speak badly of me. I want everything I say and do to be acceptable and pleasing to everyone. I don't want anyone to hurt me. I don't want anything to happen that I don't like. And I want everything to happen that I do like." Then you said, "Now, mind, figure out how to make every one of these things a reality, even if you have to think about it day and night." And of course your mind said, "I'm on the job. I will work on it constantly."

Watch your mind do this for a day. Can you see that it's trying to make everything be okay? Write about what you observe your mind struggling with when reality doesn't match your mental model of what you want.

YOU HAVE GIVEN YOUR MIND an impossible task by asking it to manipulate the world in order to fix your personal inner problems. If you want to achieve a healthy state of being, stop asking your mind to do this. Just relieve your mind of the job of making sure that everyone and everything will be the way you need them to be so that you can feel better inside. Your mind is not qualified for that job. Fire it, and let go of your inner problems instead.

Ask your mind to stop trying to make sure everyone and everything are exactly as you think you need them to be.

Complete this letter to your mind:

"Thank you, Mind, for trying to protect me. I am now ready to relieve you of the job of...." _____

_____

_____

_____

_____

_____

_____

_____

_____

_____

_____

_____

_____

YOU CAN HAVE a different relationship with your mind. Whenever it starts up telling you what you should or shouldn't do in order to get the world to match your preconceived concepts, don't listen. It's just like when you try to stop smoking. Regardless of what your mind says, you don't pick up a cigarette and put it in your mouth. It doesn't matter if it is just after dinner. It doesn't matter if you get anxious and you feel the need. It doesn't matter what the reason is—your hand simply does not touch cigarettes anymore. Likewise, when your mind starts telling you what you have to do to make everything inside okay, don't buy into what it's telling you. The truth is, everything will be okay as soon as you are okay with everything. And that's the only time everything will be okay.

All you have to do is stop expecting the mind to fix what's wrong inside of you. That is the core, the root of it all.

Observe the thoughts that are trying to control, protect, or avoid something. When they come up, say "Thank you mind for that thought, but I'm okay." and simply ignore the mind's instructions. Just notice how the thought subsides and evolves into the next thought.

Write about what happens when you change your relationship to these thoughts. Do your actions or behaviors change in any way as you allow the thoughts to pass through?

THE MIND RUNS because you are giving it the power of your attention. Withdraw your attention, and the thinking mind falls away.

Begin with the little things. For example, somebody says something to you that you don't like, or worse yet, doesn't acknowledge you at all. You are walking along and you see a friend. You say hello to them but they just keep walking by. You don't know if they didn't hear you or if they actually ignored you. You aren't sure if they're mad at you or what's going on. Your mind starts going a mile a minute. Good time for a reality check! There are billions of people on this planet, and one of them didn't say hello to you. Are you saying that you can't handle that? Is that reasonable?

Use these little things that happen in daily life to free yourself. In the above example, you simply choose not to get involved in the psyche. Does that mean that you stop your mind from going around in circles trying to figure out what's going on? No. It simply means that you are ready, willing, and able to watch your mind create its little melodrama. Watch all of its noise about how hurt you are, and how could anybody do that. Watch the mind try to figure out what to do about it. Just marvel at the fact that all of this is going on inside simply because someone didn't say hello to you. It's truly unbelievable. Just watch the mind talk, and keep relaxing and releasing. Fall behind the noise.

Watch and describe one of the melodramas your mind created today. Consider: what if you made it up—what if other people's motivations behind their actions or words are just unknowable to you? Wouldn't it be silly to have wasted all your energy on this melodrama? How much quieter would your mind be if you weren't doing this?

BEGIN THIS JOURNEY to freedom by regularly reminding yourself to watch the psyche. This will keep you from getting lost in it. Because the addiction to the personal mind is a major one, you must set up a method to remind yourself to watch. There are some very simple awareness practices that only take a second to do, yet will help you stay centered behind the mind. Every time you get into your car, as you're settling into the seat, just stop. Take a moment to remember that you're spinning on a planet in the middle of empty space. Then remind yourself that you're not going to get involved in your own melodrama. In other words, let go of what is going on right then, and remind yourself that you don't want to play the mind game. Then, before you get out of your car, do the same thing.

Try this practice of centering every time you get into or out of your car. What did you notice? Were you able to recenter and visualize yourself as part of the larger universe? If so, what did that feel like?

ULTIMATELY, EVERY CHANGE in your energy flow, whether it's agitation of the mind or shifts in the heart, will be what reminds you that you are back there noticing. Now what used to hold you down becomes what wakes you up. But first you have to get quiet enough so that it's not so reactive in there. These trigger points will help remind you to remain centered. Eventually it will become quiet enough so that you can simply watch the heart begin to react, and let go before the mind starts. At some point in the journey it all becomes heart, not mind. You will see that the mind follows the heart. The heart reacts way before the mind starts talking. When you are conscious, the shifts of energy in your heart cause you to instantaneously be aware that you are back there noticing. The mind doesn't even get a chance to start up because you let go at the heart level.

Today notice the shifts in your heart and mind.
Those are your cues to let go. See if you can relax deeply and center yourself whenever the shifts happen. Write about what you experience when you try to relax and center.

Once you've practiced this for a while, you will be able to notice the shifts in your heart and then relax before your mind even starts talking. Perhaps you've already experienced this. Write about what it is like to notice the heart react, and then let go before the mind takes over with thoughts.

ONE OF THE ESSENTIAL
REQUIREMENTS FOR
TRUE SPIRITUAL GROWTH
AND DEEP PERSONAL
TRANSFORMATION IS
COMING TO PEACE
WITH PAIN.

ONCE YOU CAN FACE your disturbances, you will realize that there is a layer of pain seated deep in the core of your heart. This pain is so uncomfortable, so challenging, and so destructive to the individual self, that your entire life is spent avoiding it. Your entire personality is built upon ways of being, thinking, acting, and believing that were developed to avoid this pain.

What are some of the ways you protect the core of your heart and avoid pain? Not letting people in? Always trying to be right? Overeating? Constantly needing to prove yourself?

What do you think would happen if you didn't do these things?

PHYSICAL PAIN IS ONLY THERE when something is physiologically wrong. Inner pain is always there, underneath, hidden by the layers of our thoughts and emotions. We feel it most when our hearts go into turmoil, like when the world does not meet our expectations. This is an inner, psychological pain.

The psyche is built upon avoiding this pain, and as a result, it has fear of pain as its foundation.

If you are doing something to avoid pain, then pain is running your life. All of your thoughts and feelings will be affected by your fears. Bring awareness to the fears that may be running your life. Write about ways you avoid feeling that core pain. Identify some of the things you do in your daily life that come from fear of psychological pain.

YOU MUST LEARN NOT TO BE AFRAID of inner pain and disturbance. As long as you are afraid of the pain, you will try to protect yourself from it. The fear will make you do that. If you want to be free, simply view inner pain as a temporary shift in your energy flow. There is no reason to fear this experience. You must not be afraid of rejection, or of how you would feel if you got sick, or if someone died, or if something else went wrong. You cannot spend your life avoiding things that are not actually happening, or everything will become negative.

How are you holding yourself back based on a made-up scenario in your mind? What is the imagined fear or pain that you are protecting yourself from? Once you identify it, practice this simple affimation. "I can handle that." Fear and pain are just something you are aware of.

Write about what it is like to affirm that you can handle pain and fear.

YOU MUST LOOK INSIDE YOURSELF and determine that from now on pain is not a problem. It is just a thing in the universe. Somebody can say something to you that can cause your heart to react and catch fire, but then it passes. It's a temporary experience. Most people can hardly imagine what it would be like to be at peace with inner disturbance. But if you do not learn to be comfortable with it, you will devote your life to avoiding it. If you feel insecurity, it's just a feeling. You can handle a feeling. If you feel embarrassed, it's just a feeling. It's just a part of creation. If you feel jealousy and your heart burns, just look at it objectively, like you would a mild bruise. It's a thing in the universe that is passing through your system. Laugh at it, have fun with it, but don't be afraid of it. It cannot touch you unless you touch it.

Practice being okay with feeling disturbance.
Today, when something happens that causes insecurity or
self-consciousness, just notice what is going on inside.

Are you able to notice the experience of discomfort
without having to figure out where it comes from,
or who's responsible, or how to control it?

Write about the experience of discomfort as just an experience— just something that happens in your life.

WHEN YOU FEEL PAIN, simply view it as energy. Just start seeing these inner experiences as energy passing through your heart and before the eye of your consciousness. Then relax. Do the opposite of contracting and closing. Relax and release. Relax your heart until you are actually face-to-face with the exact place where it hurts. Stay open and receptive so you can be present right where the tension is. You must be willing to be present right at the place of the tightness and pain, and then relax and go even deeper.

Write about a time when you were able to relax deeply and let the pain pass through. What happened when you allowed the pain in, as opposed to resisting it? How did it feel as you allowed it to pass through you?

Now, write about a time when you resisted the pain and didn't let go. How did that work out? Does your mind still think about the situation? Do similar situations cause the pain to happen again?

_____

_____

_____

_____

_____

_____

_____

_____

_____

_____

_____

_____

_____

_____

_____

_____

_____

_____

_____

_____

_____

_____

AS YOU RELAX AND FEEL THE RESISTANCE, the heart will want to pull away, to close, to protect, and to defend itself. Keep relaxing. Relax your shoulders and relax your heart. Let go and give room for the pain to pass through you. It's just energy. Just see it as energy and let it go.

When the blockages you stored in your heart are hit, notice how your heart responds. Can you feel the tug of resistance but let it go anyway? What is it like to experience your pain and blockages as energy that can pass right through you?

Limitations and boundaries

only exist at the places where

you stop going beyond. If

you never stop, then you go

beyond boundaries, beyond

limitations, beyond the sense

of a restricted self.

PART 4

GOING BEYOND

THE MORE YOU SIT in the seat of witness consciousness, the more you realize that since you are completely independent of what you are watching, there must be a way to break free of the magical hold that the psyche has on your awareness. There must be a way out.

So far on this journey, are you able to release back into the seat of awareness more often? Or, do you find yourself getting pulled back into your mind and heart? Are you doing any techniques to help maintain your distance from your inner disturbance?

Write about what you are doing and what effect it is having on your inner state.

WHAT IF CONSCIOUSNESS were to remove its focus from your personal set of thoughts, your personal set of emotions, and your limited sensory input? Would you become untethered from the bonds of the personal self and be set free to explore beyond?

You can simply witness the personal self and not get involved— you can remain in the seat of consciousness. What would it feel like to dwell in the seat of awareness? In witness consciousness, do you feel connected to something greater than what you've been watching?

YOUR HOUSE IS made of your thoughts and emotions. The walls are made of your psyche. That's what that house is.... You have pulled together in your mind a specific set of thoughts and emotions, and then you have woven them together into a conceptual world in which you live. This mental structure completely blocks you from whatever natural light is on the outside of its walls. You have walls of thoughts thick enough, and closed enough, to where nothing but darkness is inside that structure. You are so entranced into paying attention to your thoughts and emotions that you never go beyond the borders they create.

Write about what it might be like to be free of all sense of "me" and to go beyond yourself.

TRUE FREEDOM IS VERY CLOSE; it's just on the other side of your walls. Enlightenment is a very special thing. But in truth, one should not focus on it. Focus, instead, on the walls of your own making that are blocking the light. Of what purpose is it to build walls that block the light and then strive for enlightenment? You can get out simply by letting everyday life take down the walls you hold around yourself. You simply don't participate in supporting, maintaining, and defending your fortress.

Start from where you are.

With the understanding that you've built the walls of your personal self, practice being in the moment without defenses. Can you be okay with everything that comes up within you and not try to fix it?

Try to let life in by noticing sounds, colors, and people.

Take in the beauty and the ugliness. What does it feel like to let go and just be with what is, both inside and outside?

196

BEYOND IS INFINITE IN ALL DIRECTIONS. If you take a laser beam and aim it in any direction, it will go on for infinity. It would only cease to be infinite if you created an artificial boundary that it could not penetrate. Boundaries create the appearance of finiteness in infinite space. Things seem finite because your perception hits mental boundaries. In truth, everything is infinite. It is you who takes that which goes on forever and talks about a mile from here.

Right now, look at whatever is in front of you.
Now imagine the infinite number of places that exist in the Universe. Picture how expansive that is. From that perspective, is what you see in front of you any different or more important than any other place in the universe? Look in front of you; now look to the right and to the left. Is any view really more important than the others? Only the mind separates out one thing from all that is and makes it seem important or special. Can you see the truth in that?

Write about how the mind limits your experience of reality to the boundaries of your personal perception.

IF ANYTHING HAPPENS that challenges how you view things, you fight. You defend. You rationalize. You get frustrated and angry over simple little things. This is the result of being unable to fit what's actually happening into your model of reality. If you want to go beyond your model, you have to take the risk of not believing in it. If your mental model is bothering you, it's because it doesn't incorporate reality. Your choice is to either resist reality or go beyond the limits of your model.

Identify an event or situation that is challenging you presently. Write about how it does not fit with your model of what reality **should** be.

Now, write about dropping your model and accepting the event that challenges you as simply a part of reality. Like the rain; it just *exists.*

IF YOU REALLY WANT to see why you do things, then don't do them and see what happens. Let's say you're a smoker. If you decide to stop smoking, you quickly confront the urges that cause you to smoke. If you can sit through these urges, you will see what caused them. Likewise, there's a reason you overeat. There's a reason why you dress the way you do. There's a reason for everything you do. If you want to see why you care so much about what you wear and what your hair is like, then just don't do it one day. Wake up in the morning and go somewhere disheveled with your hair a mess, and see what happens to the energies inside of you. See what happens to you when you don't do the things that make you comfortable. What you'll see is why you're doing them.

Today, pick something you habitually do to feel better about yourself, and resolve to sit through the urge to do it. What comes up? Explore the sensation and write about why you perpetuate this habit.

You are
now standing
face-to-face
with ego—
note how strong
it is. Are you
stronger if you
really want
to be?

IF YOU'RE TRULY GOING BEYOND, you are always at your limits. You're never back in the comfort zone. A spiritual being feels as though they are always against that edge, and they are constantly being pushed through it. Eventually you will realize that it cannot actually hurt you to go beyond your psychological limits. If you are willing to just stand at the edge and keep walking, you will go beyond. You used to pull back when it got uncomfortable. Now you relax and go past that point. That is all it takes to go beyond. Go beyond where you were a minute ago by handling what's happening now.

Where are your limits? Write about one area you know makes you feel uncomfortable. Now, write about how you can go beyond in just this one area that you know holds you back. Can you handle the discomfort and relax through it?

IT ALL COMES DOWN TO understanding why we are clinging to our self-concept. If you stop clinging, you will see why the tendency to cling was there. If you let go of your façade, and don't try to trade it in for a new one, your thoughts and emotions will become unanchored and begin passing through you. It will be a very scary experience. You will feel panic deep inside, and you will be unable to get your bearings. This is what people feel when something very important outside does not fit their inner model. The façade ceases to work and begins to crumble. When it can no longer protect you, you experience great fear and panic. However, you'll find that if you're willing to face that sense of panic, there is a way to go past it. You can go further back into the consciousness that is experiencing it, and the panic will stop. Then there will be a great peace, like nothing you've ever felt.

That's the part very few people come to know: it can stop. The noise, the fear, the confusion, the constant changing of these inner energies—it can all stop.

Imagine what it would be like to completely let go of your entire self-concept. Are you willing to face the primal fear that caused you to build your psyche? What might be on the other side of this fear?

Imagine the peace
that you could experience
if you weren't constantly
creating and defending
your false sense of self.
Write about this.

SPIRITUALITY IS THE COMMITMENT TO GO BEYOND, NO MATTER WHAT IT TAKES. IT'S AN INFINITE JOURNEY BASED UPON GOING BEYOND YOURSELF EVERY MINUTE OF EVERY DAY FOR THE REST OF YOUR LIFE.

WHEN YOU BECOME TRULY SPIRITUAL, you are totally different from everybody else. That which everybody else wants, you don't want. That which everybody else resists, you totally accept. You want your model to break, and you honor the experience when something happens that can cause disturbance within you. Why should anything that anyone says or does cause you to get disturbed? You're just on a planet spinning around the middle of absolutely nowhere. You came here to visit for a handful of years and then you're going to leave. How can you live all stressed-out over everything? Don't do it. If anything can cause disturbance inside of you, it means it hit your model. It means it hit the false part of you that you built in order to control your own definition of reality. But if that model is reality, why didn't experiential reality fit? There's nothing you can make up inside your mind that can ever be considered reality.

Imagine for a day that when your model gets hit, you can smile, even laugh out loud as it gets hit. Rather than tightening up inside, play with responding in a new way. When it gets hit, tell yourself, "I love it when this happens!"

Write about how it feels to release the tension and laugh through the discomfort of your defenses being activated.

_____

_____

_____

_____

_____

_____

_____

YOU MUST LEARN TO BE comfortable with psychological disturbance. If your mind becomes hyperactive, just watch it. If your heart starts to heat up, let it go through what it must. Try to find the part of you that is capable of noticing that your mind is hyperactive and that your heart is heating up. That part is your way out. There is no way out through building this model of yours. The only way to inner freedom is through the one who watches: the Self. The Self simply notices that the mind and emotions are unraveling, and that nothing is struggling to hold them together.

Experiment for an entire day with being okay with everything that happens in your heart and mind. Are you able to just watch the energies inside of you that would drive you to behave in certain ways? Are you able to be comfortable with any discomfort that came up?

There is room in the Self for every experience—imagine that there is nothing you have to do about anything that comes up within you. All struggling is over and you are at peace with everything.

Write about how you perceive this state of great peace.

Deep inner release is a

spiritual path in and of itself.

It is the path of nonresistance,

the path of acceptance,

the path of surrender.

PART 5

LIVING LIFE

PEOPLE TEND TO burden themselves with so many choices. But, in the end, you can throw it all away and just make one basic, underlying decision: Do you want to be happy, or do you not want to be happy? It's really that simple. Once you make that choice, your path through life becomes totally clear.

Write about something you believe is making you unhappy. Circle any words that label this event, such as "hard" or "stressful."

Rewrite the story by choosing words that simply describe what's happening in the actual experience. Relax and release around the labels that create suffering. Breathe, and just notice the thoughts while you sit in the inner place that is witnessing the dialog. Do you see that you have the choice to simply experience life with openness?

YOU JUST HAVE TO REALLY MEAN IT when you say that you choose to be happy. And you have to mean it regardless of what happens. This is truly a spiritual path, and it is as direct and sure a path to Awakening as could possibly exist.

Make the decision that you'll stay happy and open all day today. As your day unfolds, notice what your mind is telling you about how things should be. Notice if you resist experiences and start to close. Can you relax deeply inside and be okay regardless of how things are? Write about what caused you to start closing and how you were able to open back up.

The path of unconditional happiness is a day-to-day, continuous journey of learning to stay open. Don't be discouraged if it takes time—honor every sincere attempt you make to work on yourself.

ONCE YOU DECIDE you want to be unconditionally happy, something inevitably will happen that challenges you. This test of your commitment is exactly what stimulates spiritual growth. In fact, it is the unconditional aspect of your commitment that makes this the highest path. It's so simple. You just have to decide whether or not you will break your vow. When everything is going well, it's easy to be happy. But the moment something difficult happens, it's not so easy.

Try this out with something simple that you cannot control: the weather.

Notice your reactions: Is it too hot? Too cold? Experiment with staying open by using affirmations or positive thinking, or by simply relaxing in the midst of your reactions. Relax away from the complaining mind, back into the Seat of Self.

Write about how you chose to be unconditionally happy, no matter what the weather was or wasn't.

221

THE KEY TO STAYING HAPPY is really very simple. Begin by understanding your inner energies. If you look inside, you will see that when you're happy, your heart feels open and the energy rushes up inside of you. When you aren't happy, your heart feels closed and no energy comes up inside. So to stay happy, just don't close your heart.

The best approach is to practice when you are already feeling open. The second anything happens that starts to cause you to close, relax and decide this is not something you want to trade your happiness for. Practice not closing your heart no matter what happens today.

Write about how your inner energy felt by the end of the day.

Use the moments that initially feel stressful to say, "Wow, what an amazing opportunity to relax!"

You have the power to choose to stay happy no matter what.

STRESS ONLY HAPPENS when you resist life's events. If you're neither pushing life away, nor pulling it toward you, then you are not creating any resistance. You are simply present. In this state, you are just witnessing and experiencing the events of life taking place. If you choose to live this way, you will see that life can be lived in a state of peace.

Can you see there are things in your life that you are trying to push away and others that you are trying to pull toward you? Can you see that this creates the foundation for stress and anxiety? Is it really worth it, or in most situations would it be better to simply honor the flow of life?

Write down your thoughts on this deep topic.

IT SHOULDN'T TAKE DEATH to challenge you to live at your highest level. Why wait until everything is taken from you before you learn to dig down deep inside yourself to reach your highest potential? A wise person affirms, "If with one breath all of this can change, then I want to live at the highest level while I'm alive. I'm going to stop bothering the people I love. I'm going to live life from the deepest part of my being."

If this were your last week, how would you choose to use your time?

DON'T BE AFRAID OF DEATH. Let it free you. Let it encourage you to experience life fully. But remember, it's not your life. You should be experiencing the life that's happening to you, not the one you wish was happening. Don't waste a moment of life trying to make other things happen; appreciate the moments you are given.

Today practice gratitude for the moments you are given on this earth.

Write about your experience staying open to and appreciating what you felt and observed today

_____

_____

_____

_____

_____

_____

_____

_____

_____

_____

_____

_____

_____

THERE IS AN INVISIBLE THREAD that passes through everything. All things move quietly through that center balance. That is the Tao....It is there in everything. It is the eye of the storm. It is completely at peace.

Reflect on areas of your life where you tend to swing to extremes, versus finding balance in the center. Where are you out of balance, either doing something too much, or not enough? Write about these areas of your life, so that you can begin to find your way back to harmony.

WHAT DOES IT FEEL LIKE to identify more with Spirit than with form? You used to walk around feeling anxiety and tension; now you walk around feeling love. You just feel love for no reason. Your backdrop is love. Your backdrop is openness, beauty, and appreciation. You don't have to make yourself feel that way; that is how Spirit feels. If you were asked how the body normally feels, you might say that it's generally uncomfortable about one thing or another. How about the psyche? If you were being totally honest, you'd probably say that it's generally full of complaints and fears. Well, how does Spirit normally feel? The truth is, it always feels good. It always feels high. It always feels open and light.

When you meditate or are feeling really open in your life, have you had moments when you feel untethered from your physical, emotional, and mental aspects?

How does it feel when you let go of the personal and soar upward to these higher places within your being?

LET GO OF THE IDEA of a judgmental God. You have a loving God. In truth, you have love itself for a God. And love cannot do other than love. Your God is in ecstasy and there's nothing you can do about it.

And if God is in ecstasy, I wonder what
God sees when looking at you?

What if you were able to receive love unconditionally?
Imagine being able to feel completely accepted, loved, and not judged.
Write about how this would change your life.

MICHAEL A. SINGER is author of the #1 *New York Times* bestseller, *The Untethered Soul,* and the *New York Times* bestseller, *The Surrender Experiment,* which have both been published worldwide. He had a deep inner awakening in 1971 while working on his doctorate in economics, and went into seclusion to focus on yoga and meditation. In 1975, he founded Temple of the Universe, a now long-established yoga and meditation center where people of any religion or set of beliefs can come together to experience inner peace. He is also creator of a leading-edge software package that transformed the medical practice management industry, and founding CEO of a billion-dollar public company whose achievements are archived in the Smithsonian Institution. Along with his more than four decades of spiritual teaching, Singer has made major contributions in the areas of business, education, health care, and environmental protection. He previously authored two books on the integration of Eastern and Western philosophy: *The Search for Truth* and *Three Essays on Universal Law.*

Visit **www.untetheredsoul.com** for more information.

THE INSTITUTE OF NOETIC SCIENCES

The Institute of Noetic Sciences (IONS) is a research center and direct-experience lab specializing in the intersection of science and profound human experience.

For centuries, the power of science has unlocked the mysteries of the natural world and driven human innovation. As Dr. Edgar Mitchell returned to Earth from his moonwalk on Apollo 14, he had a profound transcendence experience that led him to establish IONS in 1973. He understood that by applying the scientific rigor used in his explorations of outer space, we could better understand the mysteries of inner space—the space in which he felt an undeniable sense of interconnection and oneness. The mission of IONS is to reveal the interconnected nature of reality through scientific exploration and personal discovery, creating a more compassionate, thriving, and sustainable world.

At IONS, we are inspired by the power of science to explain phenomena not previously understood, harnessing the best of the rational mind to make advances that further our knowledge and deepen our knowing. For over four decades, IONS has provided a safe harbor for scientists and scholars to pursue research into frontier questions related to the nature of consciousness, and for healers and educators to work with emerging ideas. From our scientific exploration, we design experiential programs for personal discovery that allow each of us to access more of our human capacities and the fullness of our humanity.

Today, IONS continues to forge new frontiers in consciousness research and experiential education, developing training programs for youth, adults, elders, and professionals; all on a majestic 197-acre retreat center in Petaluma, CA, one hour north of San Francisco, CA.

Learn more and join us at noetic.org.

MORE WAYS TO EXPERIENCE
THE UNTETHERED SOUL

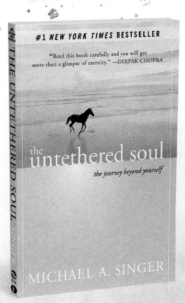